Python Programming For Beginners

A step-by-step guide to coding using python 3 for beginners to pro

Gideon Hanks

Copyright

Contents

CHAPTER 1

Introduction to python

The programming language python is a robust programming language that is interpreted, advanced high-level general-purpose language. Which was created by a developer named Guido van Rossium. The program was first introduced in 1991 and the design stressed on code readability with its usage of white space. Python language constructs and object orient-oriented approach aim more to help developers visible, clear and logical code for small and large scale project and also enterprise.

Python program is able be read by a parser. Its major benefit is that it was designed to be a highly readable language.

Python is an object-oriented programming language that helps to develop real life portable application programs.

In working with electronic devices, several or different applications are mostly in use and they are mostly developed by using different languages which the computer understands, such as C, C++, C#.

The application developed by C, C++ do not support cross platform portability. However, python is platform independence. The code reusability feature of python makes software developers to upgrade the existing applications without going to rewrite all the code of the application.

Simple program on Python;

```
def hello ()
  print ( " Hello, world!" )
```

Python source byte file extension is .py. or in advance type of .py.c

PROGRAMMING LOGIC AND TECHNIQUES

INPUT, PROCESS, AND OUTPUT

You may notice that some computer machines used in some strategic places like restaurants, shops, airline reservation counters and other various locations. At any time in this places, someone puts in a value and the computer brings out an output, which either shows on the computer screen or its being printed out on hard copy materials. To understand what happens when you key in values in the computer, this phase is called an input phase. The input values are then processed to determine the particular values; this phase is called the process phase. Immediately the process is complete, the result is either shown or displayed on a monitor or screen. This phase is well known as output phase.

PROGRAMS

Programs are a set of instructions to perform a particular job or events. For each event to be done or perform a separate program is performed. Which means to solve some real life problems, someone has to have a number of programs which sum up to form an application.

Computers are generally designed to accept and inputs, process the input and display output. Nevertheless, it has to be provided with set of instructions that states;

- The various kind of inputs will be provided
- The various kind of outputs to be expected.
- The various processing or processes to be done. Most times we use programs to
- To create pay checks
- To display or print associated reports.

HOW LOGIC OF PROGRAMS WITH CONDITIONS ARE REPRESENTED

VARIABLES AND CONSTANTS

On a normal condition the computer system has an internal memory of various sizes. This internal memory is used to store input provided by an individual or the various users, instructions to process the input, and the outcome output values. The internal memory always consists of different locations in which data is stored. After these instructions are executed, the value of the first number is accepted and stored in memory and this occurs with other value at the same time of input and stored in another location in the memory.

Variable values are mNum1, mNum2, etc...
Constant values do not change and they are assigned to a variable.
For example,
mNum1 = 15
where mNum1 is the variable,
constant is figure 15.

DATA TYPES

At times we need to enter a non-numeric data such as names and addresses of things or person. A memory space will be required in the computer to store the different data types of values.

The major data types are;

- Numeric
- Character
    - **Numeric datatypes**: These are variables that can only contain numbers like persons' age, commodity prices. It is usually used in arithmetic operations.
    - **Character datatypes**: These are variable that usually contain combination of numbers, letters, and special characters. It is usually implemented in persons or things address and also name of persons or things. On a more important note, it cannot be used for calculation even if they contain only numbers.
    - **Declaring variables**: When allocating values to memory in a program, it is very essential someone declares the variable, therefore the datatype of the variable is identified on the type of data to be stored in it.
    For example,

int mNum1 = 2.

Char mNum2.

NAMING VARIABLES

There are various guidelines in naming variables which are;

- The beginning letter of the variable always or may indicate the datatype used. For example, we make use of N or Char to signify a character or numeric as in Char Name, Nphone.
- The name of the variable must clearly describe its purpose. For example, Nresult is a numeric variable to store the score result.
- Another form is when the variable name is multiple words, each first letter of the word could be capitalized for readability. For example;

MTotalResult.

USING OPERATORS

Operators are predefined operations and tools in computer programming language.

They are;

- Arithmetic operators
- Relational operators
- Logical operators.

    - **Arithmetic operators**:

      These operators are usually used for performing arithmetic calculations I the computer system.

      The commonly used arithmetic operators are;

Multiplication	*
Division	/
Addition	+
Subtraction	-
Modulus	%

Note that the modulus operator returns the remainder value when one number is divided by another number.

    - **Relational operators**:

      These operators usually test the relationship between variables and also test the relationship between constant and variable.

      Relational operators are;

=	Equal to
>	Greater than
<	Less than

!=	Not equal to
>=	Greater than or equal to
<=	Less than equal to

- **Logical operators**:
These operators help to combine expressions containing relational operators.
Logical operators are;
  - ❖ AND
  - ❖ OR
  - ❖ NOT

  Relational operators are AND, if operator evaluates to true only all the individual conditions evaluate to true.

  mNum1 = 7 AND mNum2 > 6

  OR operator evaluates to true even if one of the individual condition evaluates to true.

  For example,

  mNum1 = 7   OR   mNum2 > 6

NOT operators is a logical operator, which evaluates to true, if the condition is not met.

For example,

NOT mNum2 <= 6

ITERATION

It is the ability of computer to execute instructions in series in a repeated number of time.

This brings flexibility of the computer to control the number of times a task is to be repeated.

This also works with the concept of loop. Which makes a loop to be defined as instructions in sequence that will be repeated more than one time.

Loop is of two types;

- Fixed loops
- Variable loops.
- Fixed loop: The fixed loop always repeats a known value.
- Variable loop: The variable loop usually repeats an unknown number of results.

CHAPTER 2

Features of python

Python is a very powerful programming language used by developer to build flexible application, and it has a powerful and useful features.

These features are;

- It is an object oriented programming language.
- Python is simple
- It is portable
- It is highly distributed
- It is very secure
- It is very robust
- It is platform independence
- It is multithreaded
- It is well structured.
- Meta programming and meta object.
- It supports functional programs.
    - **Python is object oriented:** When a program uses object that refers to real world entities, like game player or game within a class and it codes are encapsulated inside a class, and also have the characteristics of inheritance

and polymorphism, we say that program is object- oriented

- **Python is simple:** Memory allocation is easily handled in python programming language. This make the program to come to an optimum utilization.
- **Python is portable:** python has the ability to run in another computer with different operating system, and without changing the program source code.
- **Python is highly distributed:** When a program is highly distributed, it means it can be used to develop applications that can work in multiple machines, especially the internet.
Python also have the ability to support internet protocols like TCP/IP and HTML.
- **Python is very secure:** python is so secure that it has a built-in security component that allows those resources essential for its execution.
- **Python is robust:** it robust nature makes it provide features for exception handling, and memory management. This makes python unable to crash machine if minor error is encountered.

- **Python is platform independent:** When you compile a python program code, it is then converted to platform independent code, which is known as byte code.
- **Python is multithreaded:** When we say thread, it means the smallest unit of execution in python program. Program can execute simultaneously using thread.

BUILDING BLOCKS IN PYTHON

Sets of program in python consists of the following building blocks and its functionalities, which are listed below;

- Classes
- Data types
- Class members
- Packages

- **CLASS DEFINITION**

  A class can be defined as the way, manner an object behaves in a program. It comprises of variable, methods of object that share the same unique characteristics.

  Class Teacher:

Statement – 1

Statement – 1

....

....

Statement – n

Class   Teacher:

Tch_class = ' T '

Tch_name = ' Samson '

Rules or Guides taken when naming a python classes.

Errors will be noticed if this rules are not followed and they are as follows;

- Uniqueness of a class
- A class is not allowed to contain a keyword whatsoever.
- The name of a class must never have an embedded symbol like, @, !, %, &, etc….
- Python classes name should always begin with a letter, underscore (_), or the dollar symbol ($).

NAMING CONVENTIONS FOR PYTHON READABILITY

- Python class name should all form be a noun.
- Python class name in a program, the first letter should be capitalized.
- When a python name comprises of several words, especially the first letter of each word should be capitalized.

KEYWORDS/RESERVED WORDS IN PYTHON

abstract	boolean	break	class
case	catch	finally	do
return	none	continue	for
lambda	try	true	public
from	nonlocal	while	and
del	global	not	with
as	el	if	or
yield	assert	else	import
pass	except	in	raise

These are set of keywords/reserve words in Python programming language.

TYPES IDENTIFICATION

It is necessary to store and manipulate varying data while working with an application. To handle these varying data in an application when using python. Python supports various data types. Python has eight primitive data types, which are;

- Integer type
- Floating point type
- Boolean type
- Character type
    - **Integer type**: This datatype stores integer values and they comprise of
        - I. Int
        - II. Short
        - III. Long
        - IV. Byte

Int size to accommodate values are 4 bytes, range of int is -2^{31} to $2^{31}-1$, and default value is always zero (0).

Short size to accommodate values are 2 bytes, range of short is -2^{15} to $2^{15}-1$, and the default value is always zero (0).

Long size to accommodate values are 8 bytes, range of long is -2^{63} to $2^{63}-1$, and the default value is always (0).

Byte size to accommodate values are 1 byte, range of byte value is -2^7 to 2^7-1, and the default value is always zero (0).

- **Floating point type**: The floating point type usually store decimal numbers. It comprises of;
  - I. Float.
  - II. Double.

Float size accommodates 4 bytes, range of float is 3.4^{e-038} to 3.4^{e+038}, and the default value is 0.0.

Double size accommodates 8 bytes, range of double is 1.7^{e-308} to 1.7^{e+308}, and the default value is 0.0.

- **Boolean type**: Boolean types is always known to store values based on True and False, while writing a program or building an application.

CLASS MEMBERS IDENTIFICATION

Python class usually contain these various members;

- Variables

- Methods
- Objects
- Inner classes

- **VARIABLES**

  Python programs use variable to store and manipulate data, and it is used essentially as a container for storage of varying data kinds.

  Variables in python has to be declared before it will be accessed, this informs or tells the compiler about the variable type value and variable name to store.

  < variable – name > = < value >

WAYS TO ASSIGN VALUES TO VARIABLES

Python usually assign value to variable in various form. For example,

name = "writing books" # A string

height = 12 # An integer assignment

width = 25.2 # A floating point

    print (name)

    print (height)

    print (width)

Note should be taken that by default when a variable is declared in a class, but not initialized, it is assigned a default value.

RULES OF NAMING VARIABLES IN PYTHON

- Python variables name usually and must in all ways begin with a letter or underscore.
- It is very important that the keyword/reserve words should not or cannot be used as a variable name.
- Python variable names compared to machine languages are case-sensitive.
- Python variable names has the possibility of not able to contents space.
- Python variable name can only have the ability to contain alphanumeric characters and underscore, such as a-z, A-Z, 0-9, and _.

DELETING VARIABLE IN PYTHON

Python as a programming language has provided a means in which variables can be deleted from memory.

< del > = < variable – name >

CONCEPT OF LITERALS

In understanding the type of values that a variable can contain, one has to understand the concept of literals. Literal usually contains a sequence of characters like alphabets, digits, symbols that represents values to be stored in a program.

Literals could be;

- Integer literals
- Floating point literals
- Character literals
- String literals
- Boolean literals

- **Integer literal**: They are usually non-fractional numeric values. These numeric values can usually be represented in decimal, octal, and have decimal notation. Octal number are represented in proceed of zero, hexadecimal numbers are presented in prefix of 0x. integer literal representation for hexadecimal. For example, is n = 0678, while for octal is n = 0x567.

- **Floating point literal**: These numeric values usually contain a fractional part, and the floating point literals usually contain an integer and decimal part. for instance, y = 5.5 which represents a floating point.
- **Character literals**: These literals are usually represented inside a pair of single quotation mark. For instance, z = 'y'.
- **String literal**: For instance, y = " Paul " is a string literal enclosed in a pair of double quotation marks.
- **Boolean literal**: For instance, y = False is a Boolean literal that usually contain a decision of True or False remark.

METHODS IN PYTHON

Methods in python connotes or simply defined as a set of statements that is intend to specify task. Methods in python usually provide encapsulation in which data can be referred to, and also access them. It usually has method declaration and method body.

init ()

```python
            def _init_ ( School, Schair, Sbook,
Spen) :

            school.c  =  schair
            school.b  =  sbook
            school.p  =  spen
            def  messg (school):
            return ' Starting New Term '


            Eliminate_same vaariables (
serials ):

                serials = []
                if serials:
for things in serials
if things not in serials2:
                serials2 . append ( things )
else
                return serials
                    return serials2
            print ( Eliminate_same variables [
1, 2, 3, 3 ] )
```

ELEMENTS TO DECLARE METHODS IN PYTHON

- Access specifier
- Return type
- Method name

- Parameter list
- Method body
  - **Access specifier**: This is the extent to which a method will be able to have access from another class.
  - **Return type**: This usually refers to the data type of the value returned by a method. Void return type does not return value.
  - **Method name**: This is usually case sensitive and also a unique identifier.
  - **Parameter list**: A parameters are usually used to pass data to a method. Therefore, the parameter list is written between parentheses after the method name in programs.
  - **Method body**: Local variables are variables declared inside the method body and it contains set of instructions that perform various specific task.

METHOD NAMING CONVENTION

- Python method should always start with lowercase.
- Python method name should always be verb-noun combination.
- Each first letters should be capitalized if a method name contains multiple words.

```
Class teacher:
    def_init_( school, student, results )
        school.name = student
        school.score  = results
```

OBJECTS IN PYTHON

Object is regarded as an instance of a class with a unique identity. Object are distinguished from each other by their identity. Objects and class in python closely work with each other in one form or the other. An object usually contains a unique identity, while a class is usually an abstraction of related properties of various objects.

Object is usually created by declaring, then instantiate the object.

```
def class name  object name:
```

To allocate memory to the object, one need to instantiate the object to another new operator.

```
def object name = new class name ():
    y = [ [ 6, 4 ],
        [ 2, 3 ],
        [ 1, 4 ] ]
```

```python
outcome = [ [ 0, 0, 0 ],
            [ 0, 0, 0 ] ]

for m in range (len ( y ) ):
for n in range ( len ( y [ 0 ] ) ):
outcome [ n ] [ m ] = y [ m ] [ n ]
for oc in outcome :
print ( oc )
```

PACKAGE DEFINITION

When classes are grouped together, it is referred to as package, which means package is the collection of classes. It provides space that is used to organise related classes.

Package helps to coordinate classes in a program, thereby removing conflicts among classes.

init .py.

MEANS OF ACCESSING CLASS MEMBERS

These class members usually describe the characteristic behaviour of objects. They are usually hidden, protected from other class, while writing a python application program. In some case, restrictions of access to other class counter modification of data, which is information hiding or encapsulation.

USING OBJECTS IN PYTHON

Member class are usually accessed by objects. It is possible to access the data members of a class by just specifying the object name, which followed by a dot operator and the data member name.

def object name.data member name

ACCESS SPECIFIERS IN PYTHON

There are various types of Access specifiers in python that controls the access of class members.

- Public
- Private
- Protected
  - **PUBLIC ACCESS SPECIFIER**: This access specifier can be accessed by the class present within or outside the package method, public class. Data member within the class can be accessed from the class in the same package or usually outside the package.

```
def_init_ (school, student, score):
school.name = student        # public
school.results = score
```

- o **PRIVATE ACCESS SPECIFIER**: This access specifier usually creates the possibility of allowing a class to hide its member variable and methods from other classes. Which means they can be seen by outside class. So therefore, data cannot be modified or altered by any method or than member of the same class variables can only access each other in private access specifier.

```
class student:

def_init_ ( school, name, score ):

school.name = name    # private

school.results = score   # private
```

- o **PROTECTED ACCESS SPECIFIER**: This access specifier is usually implemented in inheritance where the member of a class is given the accessibility to all classes within the package and by the subclasses outside the package.

```
class student:
def_init_ (school, name, score):
school.name = name    # protected
school.results = score   # protected
```

ACCESS MODIFIERS IN PYTHON

There is list of various access modifiers in python which are;

- o Final
- o Static
- o Abstract
- o Native
- o Synchronized
- o Transient
- o Volatile

- **Final**: this access modifier is usually applicable to variables, classes and methods in a program. It must not be used with an interface in python program. During data member usage, the final represents the data member definition, that is it value cannot be modified or replaced. For example, compile-time error occurs if you try to modify the value of a variable that is declared as final. In addition, inheritance is far from usage if a class is declared final, and a method declared in program as final cannot be overridden.

```
Class school:
def_student_ ( thing, attr, value ):
    if student ( thing, attr ):
raise Exception ( " Always be hard
working " )
    thing._dict_[ attr ] = value
```

- **Static**: This access modifier is applicable to inner classes, variables and methods in a python program. The static access modifier is usually used to denote those class methods and variables belonging specifically to a class and usually non particular object in the program. The allocations are usually once. This make it notable that the static variable is not destroyed and remain available to that instance of that class when an instance of a class is destroyed.

```
Class Jumble:
Name = " jumble "
@static method
```

```python
def static ():
    print " % static () called " %
jumble.name
class offspring 2 ( jumble ):
  name = " offspring 2 "
class offspring 3 ( jumble ):
  name = " offspring 3 "
@ static method
def static ():
    print " % s static () called " %
offspring 3 . name
jumble . static ()
offspring 2 . static ()
offspring 3 . static ()


class color
    @ static method
def info ( msg ):
  print ( msg )
print ( " this class is used for representing
difficult colours. " )
    color . info ( welcome to color class " )
```

- **Abstract**: this access modifier is usually used for the declaration of those classes that define the characteristically behaviour that can be utilized in some other classes instantiation is not effective in a class being declared abstract.

Abstract is usually used with method, and it is usually declared without its implementation details. The abstract access modifier method is said to be overridden by classes that inherit an abstract class.

```
Import abc
Class shapes
   @abc . abstract method
def area ( thing ):
   pass
class rectangle ( shapes ):
   def_init_( thing, m, n ):
       thing . l = m
       thing . b = n
   def area ( thing ):
return thing . l * thing . b
 r = rectangle ( 5, 15 )
 print ( " area: ", r . area () )

from abc
```

```python
import ABC
class school ( ABC ):
def properties ( thing ):
    pass

    class secondary ( school ):
def properties ( thing ):
print ( " senior class students " )

    class primary ( school ):
def properties ( thing ):
print ( " middle class pupils " )

    class kindergarten ( school ):
def properties ( thing ):
print ( " little kids section " )

    class teacher ( school ):
def properties ( thing ):
print ( " impacting knowledge to student,
pupil and kids " )

    s = secondary ()
    s . properties ()
```

$$p = primary\ ()$$
$$p\ .\ properties\ ()$$

$$k = kindergarten\ ()$$
$$k\ .\ properties\ ()$$

$$t = teacher\ ()$$
$$t\ .\ properties\ ()$$

- **Native**: This access modifier is usually a method that modify the program compiler that method used is not written in that programming language being used, but in another programming language.
- **Synchronized**: this access modifier is a method usually used to control access in a multi-threaded programming environment. A thread can be defined as the smallest unit of execution usually within a process. Each thread usually defines a separate part in python program.

When two or more threads need access to a resource at the same time, a synchronized keyword is used as a multi-thread program.

```python
Import threading
Import time
Class atThread ( threading, Thread ):
    def_init_( thing, threadID, name, counter ):
        threading . Thread . _init_ (thing )
        thing . threadID = threadID
        thing . name = name
        thing . counter = counter
    def run ( thing ):
        print " starting procedure " + thing . name
        thread lock . acquire ()
        print_time ( thing . name, thing-counter, 3 )
        tgread lock . release ()
    def print_time (threadName, delay, counter ):
        while counter:
            time_sleep (delay )
            print " % s : % S " % ( threadName, time, counter - = 1 ctime ( time . time () ))
thread lock = threading . lock ()
```

```python
        threads = []
        thread 2 = at Thread ( 2, " Thread
-2 ", 1 )
        thread 3 = at Thread ( 3, " Thread
-3 ", 2 )
            thread 2 . start ()
            thread 3 . start ()
          threads . append ( thread 2 )
          threads . append ( thread 3 )
                for th in threads:
                th . join ()
print " important Thread Exit "


import threading
   m = 0
def increment ():
    global m
    m += 1
def thread_task ():
  for_in range ( 10000 ):
    increment ()
def main_task ():
    global m
    m = 0
```

```
p₁ = threading . Thread ( target =
thread_task )
p₂ = threading . Thread ( target =
thread_task )
            p₁ . Start ()
            p₂ . start ()
            p₁ . join ()
            p₂ . join ()
        if_name _ == " _main_ ":
for j in range ( 10 ):
            main_task ()
print ( " it should iterate { 0 }: x = { 1} ".
Format ( j, x )
```

- **Transient**: this access modifier uses a technique named serialization to save the object state in python program. It is also used to specify the object properties that can be excluded from serialization. Although, transient object properties or attributes will not be saved to disc on the system.

```
        def run ( thing, edit ):
        thing . index = thing . get_all ()
        file names = thing . get_selected (
        full_True )
        if not file names:
          return sublime . status_messages ( u "
        previous nothing " )
```

```python
fqn = file names [ 0 ]
  if is dir ( fgn ) or fgn == parent_sym:
        if not ( st3):
return sublime . status_messages ( u "
directories nothing to preview " )
thing . view . run_command ( "
directory_dired preview ", { " fqn " :
fqn 3 )
        return
if exists ( fqn ):
thing . view . run_command ( "
properties_dired_file. " { ` fqn ` : fqn 3 )
        window = thing . view . window
()
        dired . view = thing . view
        thing . focus_other_group (
window )
        window . open_file ( fqn, sublime
. Transient )
        window . focus_view (
dired_view)
else:
        sublime . status_messages ( u "
This file is total not in existence ( % s ) "
```

```python
                    % ( basename ( fqn . rstrip ( os . sep ))
                    or fqn ))

                    def set_diagnostic ( thing,
                    file_diagnostic: optimal [ Tuple ( str,
                    diagnostic ]] )
                            -> none:
                            Thing . clear ()
                            If file_diagnostic:

                    File_path, diagnostic = file_diagnostic

            View = thing_window .open_file ( file_path,
sublime . Transient )

                    if view . is_loading ():

                            sublime . set_timeout ( iambda:

                    thing . apply . phantom ( view, diagnostic )

                    thing . apply = phantom ( view, diagnostic,
400 )

        else:

                    if thing_last_phantom_set:

                        view = thing_last_phantom_set_view

                        has_phantom =
```

view . settings () get (" lsp_dignostic_phantom)

if not has_phantom:

view . settings () . get (" lsp_diagnostic_phantom ", false)

- **Volatile**: This access modifier usually update its value almost every time it is accessed. It acts as a tracker in the program. In python multi-threaded programs, volatile variables usually modify values by multiple thread intervals that cannot be determined.

```
Import threading
queue = []
m = threading . lock ()
  def n ():
global queue
m . acquire ()
queue . append ( 1 )
m . release ()
def y ():
print ( queue )
  threads [
threading . Thread ( target = n ),
threading . Thread ( target = g )
```

```
                ]
        for j in threads:
            j . start ()
        for j in threads:
            j . join ()
```

SUMMARY

- o Python program has powerful and unique features that makes it a popular and widely used programming language in the world in general and some of these powerful features are listed below;
    - It is simple
    - It is object-oriented
    - Portability power
    - Its distributive power
    - It is very secured
    - It is robust
    - It is multithreaded
- o Python program comprises of building blocks and which are;
    - It uses classes
    - Works with data types
    - It has class members
    - Works with packages
- o Class in python usually define all the characteristics and also the behaviour of an object.

- o Python keywords are usually the reserved words with unique meaning, which optimally express the features in the program.
- o The primitive data type in python are as follows;
  - We have the Integer type
  - The Floating point type
  - The Boolean type
  - And also the Character type
- o Python program Class usually have the following members in the program and which are below;
  - The Variables
  - The Methods
  - The Objects
  - The Inner classes
- o Variables in python programs is a memory location which creates room where values will be stored.
- o Object usually has a unique identity in the program and it is well known as an instance of a class.
- o Method of a program is regarded as a set of statements that usually perform specific task in various programs.
- o Constructors in programs usually initialize object of a class and also construct same object.
- o Object are usually used to access the member class of a program.
- o Packages in a program is usually regarded as a collection of classes.

- o The various types of access specifiers in python program are listed below;
    - The public access specifier
    - The private access specifier
    - The protected access specifier
- o The various access modifier in python program are below;
    - The final
    - The static
    - The abstract
    - The native
    - The synchronized
    - The transient
    - The volatile

CHAPTER 3

IMPLEMENTING OPERATORS IN PYTHON

Lots of mathematical and logical operation are don in python programming language., such as comparing and also adding numbers. In performing expression in python, multiple operators is required and it is usually in operator precedence.

X + Y is an expression;

Where X and Y are operands and "+" is the operator.

There are various types of operators in python, which are;

- Arithmetic operators
- Assignment operators
- Comparison operators
- Identity operators
- Membership operators
- Bitwise operators.

• **Arithmetic operator:**

Operator	Name of operator
+	Addition
-	Subtraction

*	multiplication
/	division
%	modulus

The modulus is used to find the reminder after dividing the two numbers.

**	exponentiation
||	floor division

- **ASSIGNMENT OPERATORS**: These operators are usually used to assign values to operators.

OPERATORS	ITS USES
=	it is a simple assignment used to assign values to variables
+=	adds two numbers and assign the result to a variable and its complex operator.
-=	subtracts two numbers and assign the result to a variable.

*=	multiplies two numbers and assign the result to a variable
/=	divides one number by another and assign the result to a variable
%=	it finds the remainder and assign the result to a variable

COMPARISON OPERATORS

OPERATORS	ITS USES
==	It acts as an equal to
!=	acts as not equal to
>	acts as Greater than
<	acts as less than
>=	acts as greater than or equal to
<=	acts as less than or equal to

These comparison operators are usually used in comparing two values and it provides an action based on the comparison.

LOGICAL OPERATORS

OPERATORS	ITS USES
and	this returns true if both statements are true
or	this returns true if one the statement is true
not	this reverse the result, returns false if the result is true

IDENTITY OPERATORS

OPERATORS	ITS USES
is	this returns true if both variables are the same object; x is y
is not	this returns true if both variables are not the same object; x is not y.

MEMBERSHIP OPERATORS

OPERATOR	ITS USES

| In | this returns true if a sequence with the specified value is present in the object; x in y. |

| not in | this returns true if a sequence with specified value is not present in the object. |

BITWISE OPERATORS

OPERATOR	OPERATOR NAME	ITS USES
&	AND	1 appears if both bits are 1
|	OR	1 appears if one of two bits is 1
^	XOR	1 if only one of two bits is 1
~	NOT	this inverts all the bits
<<	Zero fill left shift	- it shifts left by pushing zeros in from the right and let the leftmost bits fall off.
>>	Signed right shift	- it shifts right by pushing copies of left most bit in from the left, and let the right most bits fall off.

OPERATOR PRECEDENCE IN PYTHON

Operator precedence is a common thing in programming languages, especially in expression statement. In python program there are well-defined rules to specify the order in which the operators in an expression are evaluated.

Addition for instance has a lower precedence than multiplication and division.

For example, 3 *(5 + 2):

In this expression the result will become 21 as 2 will be added to 5, and then result will be multiplied by 3.

SUMMARY

- Python operators usually allows one to perform logical calculations and other mathematical calculations, like comparing numbers and as well as addition.
- In python arithmetic operations, arithmetic appends to multiplication, division, subtraction and addition.
- Python arithmetic operators are usually categorised into simple assignment and complex assignment operator in the program.
- Assigning values to variable usually works with simple assignment statement in python program.

- Complex assignment statements are usually regarded as combination of arithmetic operators and simple assignment operator. Examples are +=, -=, /=, etc…

- Comparison operator is usually regarded as two values comparison, and also perform an action on the basis of the result of that comparison. Examples are <, >, !=, ==, <=, >= etc…

- Python instanceof operator is capable of testing whether the object is an instance of a specific class at run time in the program.

- Boolean values work with logical operator evaluation and they are && and ||

- Identity operator usually use ' is ' and ' is not ' operators, where ' is ' returns true if both variable in a program are the same object. For example, x is y, while the ' is not ' returns true if both variables in the python program are not the same object. For example, x is not y.

- Python Bitwise operator are mostly used in the bit level where data are being manipulated. AND (&), OR (|), NOT (~), and XOR (^)

- Order of precedence usually goes with expression in a program that have multiple operators.

- Order of precedence are usually overridden by parentheses to get the desired results in a program.

CHAPTER 4

CONDITIONAL AND LOOP CONSTRUCTS

In python programming language, the conditional construct is said to executes block of statements in the value of the expression. When a set of statement continue to repeat, it is known as loop. It repeats or loop when it sets to true, then it terminates when become false.

THE CONDITIONAL CONSTRUCT

The conditional construct comprises of;

- The if construct
- The elif construct
- The if..else construct
- The switch construct

- **The if construct**: it executes statement in a program usually based on a specified condition. It usually supports logical conditions in expressions.

```
a = 55

b = 100

if b > a:
```

print (" b is far greater than a ")

- **The elif constucts**: it is usually used in python as a way of saying that the formal conditions in the program were set not be true.

```
a = 55
b = 55
if b > a:
        print ( " b is far greater than a" )

    elif  a == b:

        print( " a and b are said to be
equal " )
```

- **The if...else construct**: the if..else construct usually executes statements in a program on a specified condition basis.

```
a = 4
b = 400
print ( " A " ) if a > b  else
print ( " B " )
```

- **The switch construct**: this usually evaluates an expression for more than one values.

```
def switch_demo():
    Switcher  = {
    Expr_1: statement,
    Expr_2: statement,

    ..............................,

    ..............................,

    }
    Print switcher.get (argument,
    "invalid statement")
```

THE LOOP CONSTRUCT

This loop construct in python programming language comprises of;

- The for loop construct
- The while loop construct

- **The for loop construct**: The for loop construct performs while iterating over a list, the initialization statement is executed first; followed by the conditional statement and it must evaluate true, then it however terminates if the statement evaluates to false.

    Its syntax goes below;

    for iter_var in sequence:

for example;

```
print ( ' print of notes ' )
    for note in 'hello':
if note == '1':
    break
print ( note, end= " , " )
    print ( " " )

print ( ' printing notes in Hello after
omitting 1 ' )

    print ( " " )

    print (" countering block " )

    print (" just be printing " )

print ( note, end=, " )
```

The break statement in a program is a loop control statement that stops the execution of remaining statements inside the body or within the body of the loop.

- **The while constructs**: The while construct is almost similar to the for loop construction, but has a total different construct from the for loop construct.

It syntax goes below;

While condition :

For example,

Score = 1
  while score == 1 :

print (" counting from 15 to 30 ")
    count = 15
  while count < = 30:
print (count)
    count = count + 1

SUMMARY

- Python decision making technique are implemented using the following;
    - Using the if construct
    - Using if....else construct
    - Using the elif construct
- Using the if construct, program statements executes with principle of specified condition.
- Python program supports nested if construct.

- When multiple values are in play, we make use of the switch construct.
- Python supports loop constructs and which are;
    - for loop
    - while loop
    - do...while loop
        - Infinite loop can be created by using for, while and do...while loop constructs

CHAPTER 5

ARRAYS, ENUMS, AND STRINGS IN PYTHON

ARRAYS

Arrays are used to store multiple similar values in a single variable. It holds primitive datatype or object references. Array is a contagious way of storing data in variables.

ArrayIdentifierName = array (typecode, [initializers] :

ARRAY CREATION

Arrays are usually created into two types;

- One-dimensional array
- Multi-dimensional array.

■ **One-dimensional array**: This type of array usually has multiple column in a program, but has only one row in a program.

```
Import bumpy as bp
x = bp . Array ( [6, 9, 15] )
print ( x )
```

- **Multi-dimensional array**: It is usually referred to as arrays of arrays. It comprises of more than one dimensional arrays. It can have one entity which can store many records. This unique features makes it a multi-dimensional array.

ArrayIdentifierName = array (typecode, [initializer][initializer]):

x = [[8, 10, 12, 14], [9, 11, 13, 15]]

for results in x:

print(results)

x = [[8, 10, 16, 20],

[1, 2, 3, 4],

[4, 6, 8, 10]

[11, 13, 9, 7]]

For I in range (len (x)):

For j in range (len (x [i]):

Print (x[i] [j], end= " ")

Print()

ENUMS

There are predefines sets of value in a program. In order to restrict users from selecting a fixed set of predefined values, enums come to play. Therefore, Enums can be used to define a fixed set of constants.

Class Months (enum.Enum) :

Jan = 1

Feb = 2

Mar = 3

Print (" members of enum : ")

for Holidays in (months) :

print (Holiday)

STRINGS

Strings are used to store sequence of characters, like names in a record.

'strings' has same results as " strings ".

A string is usually displayed in the monitor with the function.

Print () function:

Assigning string in variable can be done as;

The variable x has a value of welcome for instance, it can be written as

x = " welcome "

print (x)

Getting the length of a string len () function can be used for instance;

a = " welcome, Dear "

print (len(a))

stg1 = ' welcome '

stg2 = ' Dear '

print (' stg1 + stg2 = ', stg1 + stg2)

print (' stg1 * 4 = ', stg1 * 4)

INHERITANCE AND POLYMORPHISM IN PYTHON

INERITANCE

This is a process that creates a new class in a program by acquiring some features from class that is already in existence.

Inheritance could be of various types;

- Single level inheritance
- Multilevel inheritance
- Hierarchical inheritance.

The single level inheritance, the single subclass usually derives its functionality of an already existing superclass in the program. Also the multilevel inheritance, subclass usually inherits the qualities and characteristics of another subclass in the program.

While the hierarchical inheritance, one or more subclasses are usually derived from a single superclass in the program.

Python inheritance can be defined as a class that most likely to inherit all the properties and methods from another class in a program.

```python
__init__()

class school :

def__init__( student, Sname, Sage) :

student . Studentname = Sname

student . studentage = Sage

def print name ( student ) :

print ( student . studentname, student . studentage )


class pentagon

def _init_ (thing, no_of_sides) :

thing . n = no_of_sides

thing . sides = [ o for i in range ( no_of_sides ) ]

def inputesides (thing) :

thing . sides = [float ( input (" Enter side " + str ( i + 1 ) + " : " ] ) for i in range ( thing . n ) ]

def dispside ( thing ) :

for I in range ( thing . n ) :
```

print (" side ", i + 1, " is ", thing . sides [i])

POLYMORPHISM

When we want to create more than one function of the same name within a class in a program, we adopt polymorphism. Therefore, polymorphism is said to be the ability to redefine a function in a program in more than one form.

Polymorphism has two types in python program, which are;

- Static polymorphism
- Dynamic polymorphism

In static polymorphism entity like method usually exist in many forms, whereby one or more methods usually exist with the same name, but in another form of argument list.

While in dynamic polymorphism for instance, if a program has a similar name or method in a subclass and superclass, a method is invoked to override the previous method, thereby providing its own implementation.

```python
Class Rectangle :

def_init_( thing, length, breadth ) :

        thing . l = length

        thing . b = breadth

def area ( thing ) :

return thing . l * thing . b


    class square

  def_init_( thing, side ) :

      thing . s = side

  def ( area ( self ) :

      return self . s ** 2

      rect = Rectangle ( 10, 20 )

      squr = square ( 10 )

    print ( " Area of rectangle is : " , rect . area () )

    print ( "Area of square is : ", squr . area () )
```

It is of huge importance to consider some vital points while implementing overriding in polymorphism and writing a python program, which are;

- It is important to note that private methods cannot be overridden, that is they are not in any way accessible in subclasses in the program.
- It is also of huge importance that final methods cannot be overridden while writing a python program.
- Caution should be taken to know that an overridden method in python program cannot be granted more restrictive access rights in a subclass of a program than it is assigned in case of a superclass.

SUMMARY

- An array is a contegeous arrangement of data in memory location.
- Elements within an array are subscript numbers and it is also called the index of the element.
- Arrays of arrays is called multidimensional arrays and comprises of multiple columns and rows.
- Enums are list of predefined values.
- Enums in python are usually declared both inside and outside a class.
- String class are used to store string literals.

- Immutable class are also known as string class.
- Inheritance can be regarded as the class that inherits the data members and methods from another class. Also known as subclass.
- We have the single level inheritance, multilevel inheritance and the hierarchical inheritance.
- Polymorphism enables data entity to exist in multiple forms.
- We have the static polymorphism and the dynamic polymorphism.

CHAPTER 6

EXCEPTION HANDLING

When a python program has been written, there need to be an exception handler that throws exception that there is run-time error in the program, so that the program will not terminate.

Here is list of standard exception in python programming language;

- Exception
- Stop Iteration
- System Exit
- Standard Error
- Arithmetic Error
- Overflow Error
- Floating Point Error
- Zero Division Error
- Assertion Error
- EOF Error
- Import Error
- Keyboard Interrupt
- Lookup Error
- Index Error
- Key Error

- Name Error
- Unbounded Local Error
- Environment Error
- IO Error
- System Error
- System Exit
- Type Error
- Valve Error
- Runtime Error
- Not Implemented Error

- Exception: this standard exception is a basic class in python for all exceptions.
- Stop Iteration: this standard exception occurs when the next () method in the python program of an iteration does not in any way point to any object in the program.
- System Exit: this standard exception occurs when there is syst.exit () function in the program.
- Standard Error: this standard exception is a base class for all built-in exception in python program.
- Arithmetic Error: this standard exception occurs for all errors during numeric calculation in the program.
- Over Flow Error: this standard exception occurs when doing calculation in the program, whereby

the calculation exceeds maximum limit for usually numeric type in python program.

- Floating Point Error: this standard exception occurs when a calculation based on floating point fails in a program.
- Zero Division Error: this standard exception occurs when there is a modulo or division by zero in numeric types in the program.
- Assertion Error: this standard exception occurs during the case of Assertion statement in a program.
- Attribute Error: this standard exception occurs when there is a case of attribute reference or assignment failure.
- EOF Error: this standard exception occurs when input () function or raw_input () and especially if the end of file is reached in a program.
- Import Error: this standard exception occurs when statement being import from library or from other files fails.
- Keyboard Interrupt: this standard exception occurs when the user tampered with the program execution, especially when the user willingly or mistakenly compresses or press ctrl + c.
- Lookup Error: this standard exception usually occurs in a program for all errors pertaining to look up and it is a base class.

- Index Error: this standard exception usually occurs in a sequence, where index is not found.

- Key Error: this standard exception occurs when a program, a specified key is not placed or found in the dictionary.
- Name Error: this standard exception occurs in a program during the local or global namespace, and are an identifier is not found.
- Unbound Local Error: this standard exception occurs when a program tries to access a local variable in a function or method, and there is no value yet to assign to it.
- Environment Error: this standard exception is a base class pertaining to all exception that raised outside the python environment.
- IO Error: this standard exception occurs especially when an input / output procedures or operation fails in a program, usually the print statement.
- Syntax Error: this standard exception occurs usually when there is an error pertaining to python syntax.
- Indentation Error: this standard exception occurs when after writing a program, a proper indentation is not specified.

- System Error: this standard exception occurs usually when python interpreter finds an internal problem, but does not exit the program.
- System Exit: this standard exception raises when python interpreter is quit by using the sys.exit () function and if not handled, this causes the interpreter to exit.
- Type Error: this standard exception occurs especially for invalid operation attempted.
- Value Error: the standard exception occurs when the arguments in a program have invalid values that is specified in the built-in function of the program.
- Runtime Error: this standard exception occurs especially when errors being generated does not fall into any category.
- **Not Implemented Error**: this standard exception occurs especially in inheritance, where an abstract method that needs to be implemented.

EXCEPTION DEFINITION

Therefore, an exception can be defined as an event that occurs during execution process in a program which usually disrupts the flow of the program instructions.

When handling an exception that are usually suspicious code that may raise an exception, so we use this two type to defend an exception handling in python exception handling, which are;

- Try: block
- Except: statement.

- **Try block**: this block usually encloses statements that might raise an exception in the program and defines one or more exception handler that is associated with it. Therefore, if an exception is raised within the block, that is the try block, the appropriate handler that is associated with it, processes it.

```
Try:
    Methods
    ...........................
except . Exception I :
    ...........................
except . Exception ii :
    else :
```

- **Except**: the except is used as an except handler. A try blocks usually have at least one except block that follows the try block, immediately. The except specifies exception type that you need to except.

```
Try:
        Cl = open ( " document ", " x " )
        cl. write ( " This is my document
for exception handling ! " )
except IO Error:
    print " Error: can \ `t find document "
else:
    print " written content in document
is successful "
cl . close ()
```

ASSERTION IMPLEMENTATION

Assertions in python are statements that states a fact boldly in your program. For instance, while writing a program containing division function, you are bold enough that the divisor should not be zero, which means the assert divisor shouldn't equal zero. It always works as Boolean expression which usually check if always return not or true. When it is false, the written program usually stops and results in throwing errors.

Assertions act as a debugging tools which bring a stop to a program when error occurred. Assertions also test a program; it tests assumptions during program execution. Assertions in python can have the following benefits, which are;

- Assertions enable one to know or confirm if the program is expectedly or working perfectly well.
- Assertions enables data validation easily.
- Assertions helps to simplify debugging and usually locate the source and the reason for the error that occurred easily.

```
assert < condition >

assert < condition >, < error message >
```

IMPORTANT NOTE IN ASSERTION IN PYTHON

- Assert statement usually takes optional message and expression message.
- They are usually the Boolean, condition in programs which are said to always come to be true in the programing code.
- Assert statement usually debug tool as it stops the python program, when there is an error occurrence.

- Assert statement usually prone to checking values of argument, prone to checking types, and also prone to checking the output of the program function.

```
def avg ( scores ):
    assert len ( scores ) != 0
    return sum ( scores ) / len ( scores )
        score1 = []
print ( " Average of score1 : ", Avg ( score1 ) )


def avg ( scores ):
    assert len ( scores ) !- o,
" list is blank "
return sum ( scores ) / len ( scores )
scores2 = [ 66, 77, 69, 80, 68 ]
print ( Average of scores2 : " avg ( scores 2 ) )
        Score1 = []
Print ( " Average of score1: ", avg ( score2 ) )


def put_drop ( commodity, drop ):
sales = int ( commodity [ " sales " ] * ( 2.0 –
drop ) )
assert 0 < = sales < = commodity
        [ " sales " ]
```

    return sales

put_drop (books, 3.0)
find (new and valid beeps):
file " < input > ", line 1, in < module >
put_drop (comod, 3.0)
file " < input > ", line 4, in put_drop
assert 0 <= sales <= commodity [" sales "]
AssertionError

put_drop (books, -0.4)

find back (new and valid beeps):

file " < input > " line 1, in < module >

put_drop (commod, -0.4)

file " < input > ", line 4, in put_drop

assert 0 <= sales <= commodity

[" sales "]

AssertionError

OVERALL / GENERAL PRINCIPLES OF TESTING AND WRITING PROGRAMS

In most cases programs in a computer don't work as expected, usually the first try doing it. Developers or programmers usually make mistakes, which are usually errors from typing while writing the program, most keywords are not understood by the program. Debug is a technique used restore the program when something goes wrong while programming.

In overall, programs being written that another programmer cannot understand or comprehend usually has imperfection in it.

Thinking goes with program, in a real sense, when a programmer or programming team has awaiting problem to solve to make things easy, they usually find a way to design the program in form of a prototype by thinking of countless methods problem solution need to be found, other than immediately sit down somewhere and start typing in code, which will not be appropriate.

An unplanned program before coding will not work before a planned program. A planned program executes properly, while an unplanned program will be written in and usually compiled faster, but it's just a first step of creating a program that will work. This follows by the debugging stage of the codes written. In a vast majority of time, planned program usually has few bugs in the codes compared to the unplanned program.

In a more parlance, planned programs are usually more structured and styled compared to the unplanned programs. Planned programs bugs are usually easily seen.

HOW DOES ONE DESIGN A PROGRAM BEFORE CODING?

One of the most common technique used to design is called top-down design. This design technique called top-down usually divides the program into various sub-tasks. These are problems that need to be solved which is the sub-task. They are usually solved using algorithm, implementing of function and data in the program algorithm.

This top-down design technique serves some few purposes and they are;

- Ensure that you understand and comprehend how the algorithm works, if you are unable to trace the algorithm; it is impossible to write a program to implement it.

- Top-down design usually checks out the algorithm to see if it will be effective on the given problem. If it is not effective, you can start looking for another algorithm to work with.
- Top-down design gives you the detail effectiveness of a short, easy run of the algorithm that can be of great usage when debugging the code in the program.

PROGRAMMING BEING STRUCTURED

Testing a program separately, it has to be structured and divided into sub units, which brings a great advantage when debugging the program. when codes are in sub unit, they will be separated from other program for debugging. Debugging will be much harder when no debugging is performed during the code writing in the program. This makes it complex, thereby making one to search for bugs in the entire program. So if the program sub units are debugged on its own, the program source code that must be traced to debug is smaller.

Debugging becomes easier when storing the sub unit of a program into separate source files.

PROGRAM COMPILATION AND COMPILATION ERROR

Compiling a program is usually the first step after typing in a program or a sub unit of a program. This process usually converts source files in the program typed into the computer and are placed in an object file " stored ". This process is well known in a computer program as compiling.

PROGRAM COMPILER ERRORS

Powerful and non-powerful programming languages have syntax rules that governs it. These rules determine the legality of statements in the programming language. Compiler is usually built in a programming language, which makes it a necessity to enforce these rules.

The compiler prints or informs the system that there is a rule breakage, thereby not letting an object file to be created in the program. Scanning source file error continues with the computer and reports other form of errors found. Sometimes, the compiler gets confused by reporting perfect statement as error found, which brings us to the rules that governs it.

These rules are as follows;

- First rule of compilation errors
- Second rule of compilation errors

- **First rule of compilation error**: the beginning computer code error is usually a true error, while the later errors may not be true errors in the computer program. Most times the follow errors usually leave or clear when the beginning error is erased. If other errors are springing up, decline them and fix the errors confirmed to you to be sure, then recompile the program. Those errors may willingly clear of when the errors you are sure of are deleted. Compilers are created by human beings and they are programs. The error messages it usually shows may be confusing or sometimes totally wrong. Actual errors usually do not reside on the line of the error messages in the program. Source files are being scanned from top sequentially to the bottom in a program code. Errors are not quickly detected by the compiler until lots of lines under where the actual error is located. Usually, the computer does not realize this in the program and then refers to the line in source file of the program, where it detects something has gone wrong. Errors that are true are usually earlier in the code.

- **Second rule of compiler errors**: Errors during program compilation are sometimes caused by any source code line above the line referred by the compiler; but it can never be anyway caused by a line below upper line in the programming code. An effective way for finding the cause of confusing compiler errors is to remove or delete or better still comment out following section of code until the errors does not appear in the program. When the error does not appear again, the last section in the program code must have being the error for the program not to function properly. warning notification is usually done by compiler. These warnings are logical errors in the program and not syntax error, which signifies a statement in your program to be legal, but doubtful. When warning is generated, it should be treated as errors. At times computers are normally set to different levels of warning in the program. It is usually a high advantage to set this level as possible in order for the compiler to give as many warnings. A program is syntactically correct when the program codes is compiled with no error found in the lines of code, but does not mean that the program itself is correct. Although the program may still have many logical errors in the codes. Therefore, an English paper statements or words may be grammatically correct as in verbs, pronoun, etc.., but totally gibberish to the compiler.

One difficult bug to discover in the program code occurs when there are two definitions of global variable or function. In some cases, there are bugs related to the linker, where the linker usually picks the first definition it finds and leaves the remaining ones. Most linkers usually show a warning message when bugs discovery occurs.

RUNTIME ERRORS

Termination of computer programs by the compiler usually occurs when there are run-time errors in the program. Therefore, a run-time error is an abrupt stop of a program in execution process.

DEBUGGING IN PROGRAMS

In order to debug a program one has to start with a problem, create an avenue to examine the source of the problem, and then make amends to it or fix it. Therefore, debugging is the process of fixing, amending errors in program code. When being told by someone that he or she has debugged a program. It simply means that he or she has fixed the constraint in the program, or the bug is no longer in existence.

SUMMARY

- An exception is thrown when a run-time error occurs in the program.
- The concept of enclosed statement that may raise exception is usually the try block in a program.
- A try block goes with the except in exception handler.
- As per the application requirements, customized exception can be created.
- In python program the statements that enable someone to test assumptions that one makes regarding execution in program is Assertion statement.
- assert keyword is used to implement assertion in python program.
- Designing a program before coding ensure proper understanding of how the algorithm works and top-down design method.
- Program compiler usually has two rules that governs it, and which are;
  - First rule of compile errors.
  - Second rule of compiler errors.
- Debugging is the process of fixing, amending errors in program code.

ABOUT THE AUTHORS

Gideon Hanks is a programmer who understands python programming language and their application to 21st century problems. Gideon has over 15 years experience in programming and writing on the latest gadgets and technical appliances that uses Python Programming Language. He values making an impact has a podcast where he teaches newbies the nitty-gritty of Programming Python..

Gideon holds a Bachelor's degree in Computer science and Engineering from the University of Toronto, Canada. He is happily married with three beautiful daughters.

www.ingramcontent.com/pod-product-compliance
Lightning Source LLC
Chambersburg PA
CBHW072109150726
47999CB00005B/1972